An A-Z of Tricky Behaviours in the Early Years

by
Dr Hannah Mortimer

Acknowledgement
The staff, children and parents of Thornaby Pavilion Playgroup who hatched the
plan for 'Ditching their dummies'.

A QEd Publication

Published in 2006

© Hannah Mortimer

ISBN 978 1 898873 03 7

British Library Cataloguing
A catalogue record for this book is available from the British Library.

Published by QEd Publications, 39 Weeping Cross, Stafford ST17 0DG
Tel: 01785 620364
Website: www.qed.uk.com
Email: orders@qed.uk.com

Printed in the United Kingdom by J.H. Brookes (Stoke on Trent).

Contents

Introduction

The aim of the book

We all have to deal with tricky behaviours in young children from time to time and have probably wished that we could reach for a recipe book or a magic wand. However, we also realise that all children are individuals and need our creativity and expertise in designing approaches that are tailor-made for them. This is because *how* we deal with the behaviour depends on *why* children are doing it in the first place. This book will start you off with plenty of imaginative ideas for managing some of the more common tricky behaviours you are likely to find in a nursery group, crèche, playgroup or childminding setting.

This book sits alongside another book in this series, *Behaviour Management in the Early Years* and helps you put the ideas of behaviour management into practice when managing a whole range of behaviours that children in their early years display. The companion book gives you a framework for thinking about young children's behaviour and how to encourage children to behave appropriately when this becomes a problem. It provides you with the general approaches that you need in order to manage behaviour in the early years. However, this book deals with specific behaviours such as biting, kicking or throwing temper tantrums.

Why have more than one book? This is because it is impossible to provide 'recipe book' approaches for 'solving' behaviours. Each behaviour is specific to the child, the situation and how that behaviour is being handled. Each behaviour also carries its own message about the child and their experiences and the best approaches are going to be those planned individually based on your own observations and knowledge of the child. Two books give you a mixture of recipes but also the *understanding and reflection* to enable you to do your own 'cooking'. That way, you can plan your behavioural approaches more individually.

Some settings have found it helpful to hold one copy of the general book to be used during training sessions for all staff and also and by the manager

4

or special educational needs coordinator (SENCO) when planning behavioural interventions for children with additional needs. At the same time, they have found it helpful to make sure that each room leader has a copy of this specific 'A-Z' for day-to-day ideas when managing more typical behaviours. This book will sit most comfortably within the framework of what we know about how young children learn, develop and behave if staff members also have a basic knowledge of and training in the approaches developed in the companion book.

Who the book is aimed at

This book will be helpful for early years practitioners, childminders, early years and foundation stage teachers, managers, SENCOs and support teachers. Parents and carers will find many of the approaches very relevant to their own situations and might find it useful to use the same strategies as in the nursery setting. All the examples relate to children aged one to four.

How to use the book

The book is divided into two sections. At the beginning you will find a short section which gives you a set of principles for managing children's behaviour in the early years. There then follows an A-Z covering typical behaviours that you may find yourself dealing with in your day-to-day work with young children. Each has a brief pen picture of a child displaying that kind of difficulty, how staff worked out what to do, what they did and why it worked. You will find that the approaches used fit with what you will have learned from those described in *Behaviour Management in the Early Years*. You will find sections on:

- Biting
- Bossing
- Climbing
- Crying
- Ditching the dummy
- Kicking and smacking
- Lack of confidence

- Not doing as asked
- Pulling and tugging
- Running off
- Scratching and gouging
- Soiling
- Spitting
- Swearing
- Temper tantrums

Principles

It helps if you and your colleagues share some basic principles and visions concerning your work with young children's behaviour. Here are some examples to get you going.

Guiding Principles

1) We encourage the children to behave appropriately using positive approaches which encourage their self-esteem.

2) We manage the children's behaviour with a proper respect for the children themselves and their parents or carers. We respect their culture, their ethnicity, their language, their religion, their age and their gender. The approaches we use for managing behaviour must be respectful of all children regardless of their gifts, abilities or specific learning needs.

3) Behaviour management and the personal, social and emotional education of young children are not two separate, discrete activities. As a consequence, when we work with young children's behaviour, we will attend to their whole development and lives and not to certain aspects of it.

4) We believe in the principle of the 'loving use of power'. Early years educators inevitably have power; this needs to be acknowledged and used lovingly, wisely and well.

5) The interests of the child are paramount. Changing their behaviour must enhance their lives, their learning and their development. It must 'work' for the child.

6) We also recognise that children will thrive best only if their families thrive and we aim to work in close partnership with families and the community.

If you are going to put these principles into practice, then there are key things that you need to acknowledge.

- Each and every child is entitled to follow a full and balanced Early Years Foundation Stage framework and that it is up to early years workers to plan approaches and interventions that are going to make this possible.

- All practitioners should follow an inclusive approach in which children are not excluded on account of their behaviour.

- Children need to feel positively about themselves if they are to behave well and we therefore need to adopt positive approaches for managing their behaviour.

- Children behave according to their ages, stages and particular experiences. Our expectations have to be set accordingly.

- All behaviour takes place in a context. There is, therefore, something which will have led up to and triggered the behaviour, be it in the environment or from within the child's previous experiences.

- There will also be a certain consequence of the behaviour which will affect whether that behaviour is likely to happen again.

- Armed with this knowledge, you can plan changes in settings or responses in order to change a difficult behaviour.

- You need to create the right ethos for appropriate behaviour by helping the children to feel settled, secure, entertained and relaxed. They will respond best to clear routines with the opportunity to make choices within the safe boundaries that you set them.

- You need to work on building your own personal relationship with each child as an individual, sharing talking, humour, play and peaceful moments too.

- Your approaches should be flexible to allow for individual differences, temperaments and personalities.

- There are no problem children – only problem behaviours.

- All interventions that are additional or different to normal should follow a period of assessment and observation in which you look for the child's strengths, difficulties and the context for those difficulties.

- The approaches in this book often suggest basing your observations on a S.T.A.R. assessment (based on the Basic Portage training workshop, see www.portage.org.uk for further information). This means using observational methods to gather information about the **Setting** (what happened before the behaviour took place, the context, the situation at the time), the **Trigger** (what seemed to set the behaviour off), the **Action** (exactly what the child did) and the **Response** (what happened as a result of the behaviour or what those around the child did next).

- If you are planning an intervention that is additional or different to your usual day-to-day approaches, you should always find a way of involving parents and carers fully in your planning and interventions.

- As a general principle, try to keep families closely in touch with your policies and approaches for managing behaviour so that you can share the results and achievements together.

Tricky behaviours

Biting

Pen picture

Kieran is 20 months of age. He has settled happily into his day nursery which he joined two months ago. Recently, Kieran has started to bite other children. At first, staff thought this would be a passing phase, but the behaviour is becoming worse. He seems to make a beeline for certain children and, unless he is caught in time, will bite so hard that it draws blood. Other children are becoming frightened of Kieran and do not want to play near him. Other parents are beginning to complain.

How staff worked out what to do

Staff decided to start with an observation of when the attempts to bite were at their worst. An extra pair of hands was arranged so that one of them could become an observer for an hour. Kieran's regular helpers were asked to watch out for him and step in using their usual approaches if he attempted to bite.

They noticed that Kieran was happy to play alone, but was not happy when other children approached or tried to share his toys. This is when he would attempt to bite. He would also bite if he wanted a toy that another child was already holding – especially if he knew that they would not resist.

Staff used their general observations and Trackers records (see page 40) and noted that there were no other concerns about his development which appeared to be ahead of his age in everything except social skills and social interaction. His language was coming on well though he sometimes became impatient with himself.

After sharing their concerns with Kieran's parents, staff realised that Kieran had not had many experiences of playing socially with other children in the past. Kieran is the only child in his family and was described by his parents as 'a determined character'.

What they did

Staff members decided to do two things. They decided to plan activities that would be enjoyable to Kieran in which they played alongside him with one other child. They chose activities that were more fun when played with more than one child and taught Kieran how to share, take turns and ask for things. Staff did this by giving clear instructions, showing him what to do as well as telling him and using strong praise and enthusiasm when he followed the rules.

At other times of the day, they decided to watch him carefully and step in to reiterate the simple rules if another child approached his play. If he attempted to bite, they gave a clear 'no biting', spoken with firmness and confidence but no anger. He was then moved apart from the other child who was comforted. Kieran would then be helped to say 'sorry' (his helper would say it for him at first) and redirected on to another activity.

Why it worked

Children bite for many reasons – anger, frustration (especially if they cannot yet talk) because it 'works', because it gets them attention, because they enjoy it, because they are teething or hungry and even out of passion.

The observation helped staff work out that Kieran was biting because he didn't know how to share or ask for things nicely, and that he hadn't yet learned the benefits of playing socially. Rather than give him plenty of attention for the biting, they set up activities that would be even more interesting and used these to actually teach Kieran how to play socially. Had they tried to manage the behaviour using negative means – nagging him or being cross – Kieran, being a determined child, might have continued with the behaviour 'just to keep life interesting'. When he did try to bite, he discovered that more attention went to the other child, and that saying sorry meant that everyone could move on.

Bossing

Pen picture

Jojo is three and loves to organise everybody. She is always first to join in activities though her attention span is still quite short and she is quickly distracted by what is going on around her. The problem is that she will often interfere with other children, especially those younger or smaller than herself. She will try to lift them bodily towards what she wants them to play with and will not take 'no' for an answer. She can become quite angry and impatient with children who will not play her games.

How staff worked out what to do

Staff realised that this was a rather general problem and difficult to define. So they started by discussing Jojo as a team and deciding more clearly what the problem was. They decided that Jojo had a difficulty in listening to others and taking on board what they said. She also had a tendency to take over another child's play without first negotiating with them.

The staff kept a diary record for a fortnight in order to observe more closely how Jojo was playing. They recorded incidences where she managed well without demonstrating the problems, and incidences where she did not. They also talked to Mum who explained that Jojo was the oldest of six cousins who lived close by and never resisted her.

They decided that Jojo needed help to negotiate more when she played with others and to understand another's point of view. They also felt that all the children needed help to become assertive and to think about feelings. Finally, they thought that Jojo would benefit from more work on the skills of looking, listening and holding attention.

What they did

Staff planned a multi-pronged approach. They introduced a regular music circle time (see page 40) to help the children see each others as individuals, develop their confidence and assertiveness in a group and develop looking and listening skills. Jojo was given specific praise for joining in so well – for looking, listening and waiting her turn in the circle.

During story time, puppets were introduced and used to act out scenarios that mirrored what the staff were trying to teach Jojo. Jojo was also given little jobs of responsibility to do in which she could appropriately take the lead and help to organise others – handing out the snacks, helping to tidy up and showing another child how to work the computer. One member of staff was allocated to support Jojo for ten minutes per session, helping her decide who she wanted to play with and then showing her how to negotiate entry to their play. This work was followed up throughout the rest of the session by stepping in and supporting Jojo when she wanted to play with somebody else.

Why it worked

During circle time, each child can respond as an individual despite being part of a large group and it can be an excellent way of teaching interpersonal skills. Jojo had never stopped to think about why other children might wish to object to her advances – indeed she did not stop to think about much at all as she played and flitted between activities.

As she learned to extend her attention a little, she could understand what her helper was explaining to her and she began to really enjoy putting her new skills into practice. The little jobs of responsibility made her feel valued and important. She loved the puppet play and spent happy hours teaching the puppets how to behave in a friendly way! Staff members were careful to catch Jojo being friendly and use specific praise to let her know that she was doing well.

Climbing

Pen picture

Mark is one and has just learned to trot and climb with confidence. Since learning how to climb upwards, this has become his principal delight and his childminder is concerned that he will fall from a cupboard or windowsill and hurt himself. This is because he seems to want to climb the whole time. Mark is doing well in all areas of his development and is happily settled with his minder. Mum and Dad say that he is just the same at home and that they do not mind him climbing on their sofas so long as he is safe.

How his childminder worked out what to do

The childminder decided to start with a bit of detective work. She decided to carry on handling the climbing in just the way she always had, but to take a note of what she was doing. She decided that it would be wrong to see this as a 'problem' behaviour since climbing was a natural step in his development. At the same time she needed to make sure that his climbing was appropriate and did not take place on certain furniture or where it was not safe. So she asked herself what it was that was keeping the behaviour going.

She was interested to note that she always handled it in a certain way. She would call to him in a cheerful voice: 'Mark – you're at it again, *down* you come', lifting him down to the ground at which point he would trot away laughing. It occurred to her that (a) Mark needed plenty of opportunities to climb safely and (b) Mark thought that the whole ritual of lifting him down was a wonderful game. She worked out that distraction was a far better method of bringing him down to ground level and she started to look for activities that would be just as motivating for him as the constant climbing.

What the childminder did

His childminder made sure that Mark got outside whenever possible during his sessions with her. They would take a trip to the local park where there were safe toddler slides and climbing frames. If it was rainy, she would set up a tumble area in the sitting room with cushions, an indoor climbing frame and some cardboard boxes to clamber over. She decided to use distraction as the main method of restricting any inappropriate climbing.

As he began to ascend, she brought out a particular toy or drew his attention to something interesting to see. If he ignored this, she would give a clear instruction: '*Down* please', issued with a firm voice and a helping hand to climb down again himself. Warm praise was given when he landed down again. Mark was also given a safe platform at the 'waving goodbye window'.

Why it worked

When you stand back to observe behaviour, you often find that it follows a regular pattern. Here, the childminder worked out that Mark was seeing the climbing and lifting down as a game to be played over and over again. She broke the pattern by making sure instead that his attention was caught by something interesting at ground level.

Mark was taught how to climb down safely and his childminder made sure that his need to climb and develop his new found skills of moving and balancing were catered for in appropriate situations. When she needed to, she used a clear, firm voice so that Mark knew that it was not a game. Instead of telling him what *not* to do ('No climbing please'), she gave positive information about what Mark *should* do ('Down please').

Crying

Pen picture

Liberty is four and, despite having been in nursery for over a year, still cries frequently, especially when her mother drops her off or collects her. Liberty's mother has found this very difficult and is clearly anxious about her. When she is occupied and busy, Liberty mixes well and seems fairly confident in her interactions with other children. However, if things do not go her way, she tends to cry loudly and cling to a member of staff.

How staff worked out what to do

Liberty was a bit of a mystery; despite being so tearful, she could also present as a confident child and there were times when she showed that she really enjoyed her nursery.

Staff members decided to start with an observation, recording when Liberty appeared to be most upset, what triggered it, how long she was distressed and what brought her out of it. First of all, it was evident that the worst time was when Liberty first arrived in the morning when she would cling to her mother and shout tearfully. At the same time, Liberty's mother looked anxious and gave her daughter a great deal of attention for this behaviour. Staff also noticed that if they distracted Liberty quickly, once her mother had left, Liberty settled happily and soon forgot to be upset.

It occurred to staff members that Liberty and her mother did have some separation anxieties and they were probably fuelling each other's anxiety. If Liberty cried later in the session, she always did so 'at' an adult, as if expecting attention and help straight away. Because she was so settled otherwise, staff began to wonder if some of Liberty's crying was a learned behaviour and that they should help her to take more initiative in sorting out her own woes.

What they did

First of all, staff members worked on Liberty's separation anxiety. They asked her mother to send her in with something interesting to show her key person to bridge the gap between arrival and settling in. They also invited Liberty's mother to peep through the window to see just how quickly she settled – this was an eye opener to Mum and made her less anxious herself.

Liberty's key person planned the first quarter of an hour carefully each session, making sure that there was something interesting to distract Liberty until she had settled in. Incidences of loud tearfulness were handled calmly by leading her to a cushion to comfort and calm herself, then using strong praise as she quietened. She was given a small bottle to fill with her tears for Mummy – and found she could not! A colourful sticker chart was used to celebrate sessions when she had not had to cry.

Why it worked

Transfer objects – something interesting to carry in and show or a cuddly toy from home – are useful ways of helping children bridge difficult transitions in their day and separate more easily. Distraction works beautifully in helping sensitive children to settle, especially if combined with a quick cuddle and a confident approach.

It might have been that Liberty's crying always led to high-level attention and enquiry from others and no-one before had rewarded her for not crying. Because staff combined this with showing her how to solve her problems, she actually learned new ways of coping. The tear bottle approach is one example of a family therapy method called 'paradoxical injunction' – sometimes, if you permit an undesirable behaviour, it can actually decrease it. However, this approach should not be over-used!

Ditching the dummy

Pen picture

Daisychain Day Nursery staff decided that it was time to do something about dummies. Whilst they were well used to making provision for their younger children who had dummies, they had noticed that several of the three and four year-olds insisted on having their dummies as soon as their parents or carers turned up and that this was actually getting in the way of their talking and language development. The matter was flagged up at a staff and parents' meeting and both sides decided to take a united stance!

How staff worked out what to do

Staff and parents had recently shared a joint training event with a speech and language therapist and picked up plenty of ideas for language development. When discussing these ideas, it had emerged that many parents found it very hard to persuade their older children to give up their dummies. Staff members decided that a group approach would be helpful, especially if they shared what they were doing with parents and carers so that their work could be followed through at home. They decided to use their regular circle time as a place to discuss dummies together.

What they did

Staff members introduced the children to a large puppet, Polly, at circle time. Polly happened to have a large dummy in her mouth and sat shyly, watching the children. On Day 2, the children were curious to talk with her and the adult suggested that they tell her their names. When they asked her questions, Polly gave muffled replies, her mouth full of dummy. On Day 3, one of the children suggested that Polly take her dummy out of her mouth and they all cheered as she became brave enough to do so!

That session, the children made and decorated a wonderful 'tree' using a branch and glitter. The adult explained that this was a magic dummy tree and invited Polly to hang her dummy on the tree. Polly did so with the children's help. The next day the dummy had turned into a little teddy bear! Polly was delighted. One of the children asked if it would work for him and the adult suggested he try.

As the week progressed, all the children brought in their dummies for the tree and were rewarded with teddies! Parents and carers joined in the fuss and celebration and everyone went home delighted. That is, all except one little boy. The staff member (pre-briefed by Mum) wondered if his dummy hadn't worked because he had 10 more at home? This was indeed the case and the next day he gladly brought them all in and benefited from the magic too!

Why it worked

Joint training events with both parents and staff are excellent ways of developing ideas together and working in partnership. This approach would not have worked unless both sides had worked together. Children often need a 'context' for change so that there is a purpose and a framework – the magic dummy tree and the puppet Polly served to make the children feel involved and distract them from the potential battleground of ditching the dummy.

Narratives and stories are a powerful way of helping children to think about behaviour and engage with change. This was such a creative and imaginative approach, delivered with confidence and panache, that it was bound to impress the children deeply.

Kicking and smacking

Pen picture

Will is four and is described as a child who learns very quickly and likes to be in charge of himself and other people. He is happy to come to nursery and joins in all the activities though often elaborates them to make them more challenging or interesting. Inexperienced staff members find him rather disconcerting as he questions their authority and can be quite domineering, telling them what he wants them to do and refusing point blank if he does not wish to comply with a request. The problem lately is that he has begun to hit and kick other children and does not appear to care that he is hurting them. Sanctions do not seem to work and he can refuse to go to 'time out'.

How staff worked out what to do

Staff had seen this kind of challenging and questioning behaviour in other children who were very bright and already knew that they had to keep him challenged and stimulated, 'going with him' and his ideas as long as it was appropriate and making the most of his considerable strengths.

At the same time, however, they realised that he had to learn how to share the limelight and how not to impinge on the freedom and comfort of others. They were worried about the anger in his reactions to others and found this difficult to share with parents as they had noticed Dad react angrily to Will at the school gate.

The fact that he knew perfectly well how to behave, but was choosing to behave aggressively, was also very worrying to them. Staff members realised that a positive approach would be needed and that they somehow had to find someone who was a 'match' for Will and for whom Will would want to behave better.

What they did

The manager met with parents, emphasising the positive target ('Will is such a clever boy . . . we need to teach him how to get on with others so he can make the most of his time at nursery. How do you make sure he is kind at home?').

It was decided that the most experienced member of staff should become Will's key person. This staff member had attended in-service training on extension work for bright children and knew some of the methods for intriguing and challenging children like Will. He gave Will a set of clear rules as to how to behave, making it clear what would happen if Will followed them (five minutes on the school computer at the end of the day) and what would happen if not (four minutes boring 'time out' away from the action). Will was taught a simple breathing technique for reducing his angry feelings (by imagining he was a tightly filled balloon, liable to whiz out of control, and letting some of his air out slowly). New activities were often shared with Will first so that he could then show the other children what to do.

Why it worked

It was perfectly reasonable for staff members to match personality of key person to child – Will needed a strong 'match' who could stay one step ahead of him. The approach used was far wider than simply controlling his behaviour and involved meeting his intellectual needs as well, thereby giving him reasons for wanting to behave better. Showing other children what to do and helping them gave him social prestige and was more appropriate than dominating them.

Approaches were shared with the family so that they saw his strengths as well as his weaknesses and stopped modeling aggressive smacking or shouting – Will had learned that when something really mattered or you felt angry, you simply smacked like Dad did. Needless to say, staff continued to monitor the home situation because of their duties under Child Protection procedures.

Lack of confidence

Pen picture

Daniel is three. He started at nursery a term ago but is still extremely shy. He still cries whenever his nana drops him off and continues to sob or to cling to one of the helpers for the first half-hour or so. Even then, he remains very quiet and withdrawn and never joins in at group time. He is timid of anything new and cries if demands are made on him or if the group becomes noisy.

How staff worked out what to do

Staff members were very concerned and asked the special educational needs coordinator (SENCO) of the attached school for general advice. She suggested a period of observation to begin with, trying to tease apart what was making Daniel so upset. This helped staff members to hatch the hypothesis that Daniel's *confidence* was very low. They could see that he was a shy little boy and this was not surprising because his mother and his grandmother were also quiet and shy. Staff accepted that this aspect might not change, but that they could certainly help Daniel to feel more confident within the group and to play sociably with the other children.

Staff members knew that confidence and feeling successful were linked together. They also knew that children who made positive attachments within the group would feel more secure and more willing to explore and to 'have a go'.

What they did

They started off by allocating a key person to act as Daniel's 'secure base' within the group. They suggested that he arrive a little earlier than the other children so that he could come in quietly and settle in before the livelier children arrived. His key person stayed close to him until he had settled in and began to share with him ways of playing that he found fun and successful. She used very strong praise and a gentle, closely interested approach that made him feel valued. His key person also supported his play the rest of the session, moving close to encourage when she felt it was needed or involving him in small group play. During group time, she made sure that he was sitting with her and involved him by asking him directly and then relaying his contribution to the wider group.

Story times for Daniel were always held in a small group in the story corner until he became more used to coping in the large group. Finally, they used a Music Makers circle time (see page 40), once again with the key person sitting beside Daniel to encourage and support him.

Why it worked

The more willing children are to 'have a go' and the more often they succeed, the more confident they become. For very shy children, or for children with separation difficulties, this can be quite a problem – they are too distressed to 'have a go' and therefore cannot break the cycle of low confidence. Staff members made use of 'attachment theory' to solve this problem – children who can become attached to a key person within the group can join in better and begin to feel successful learners. It did not matter that Daniel became 'a little shadow' to his key person – this was the natural next step for him in overcoming his low confidence.

Not doing as asked

Pen picture

Molly is nearly three and is very contrary. When asked nicely to do something, it feels to staff members as if she automatically wishes to do the opposite. This is getting in the way of her enjoying her time at nursery as she tends to opt out of some of the exciting learning and play opportunities on offer. If pressed, Molly tends to throw a tantrum or sulk. She enjoys adult company and also enjoys playing with the other children on her terms.

How staff worked out what to do

Staff needed to stand back and observe why Molly appeared to find it so difficult to do as she was asked. First they checked her understanding – could she actually *hear* and *understand* what she was being asked to do? Short spells of one-to-one play convinced them that she could, though they noticed that her attention was not always captured the first time they spoke to her.

Then they carried out a S.T.A.R. analysis (see page 9), noting times when she complied beautifully and times when she did not. They found that she was a little girl who needed to feel in control of her session and opted out if she was not sure what was coming next. They talked to her parents who said that Molly showed a similar pattern at home. For the sake of peace, they often let her get away with it. Staff hatched the hypothesis that Molly's behaviour had not always been handled with consistency and she had not yet learned that when adults say something they mean to carry it through. She was also a little girl who liked to know what was happening next and used her non-compliance as a means of escaping things she was not too sure about.

What they did

One of the staff members helped Molly take a series of photographs of all her favourite activities at nursery. These were made into laminated cards to use as a choice selection for Molly to decide what she would like to do next. Whenever there was a change of activity, Molly was warned first ('After snack-time, it will be time for . . .' or 'When we have tidied up, then . . .').

When staff had to ask Molly to do something, they engaged eye contact first and got down to her level. They spoke her name and gave the instruction simply, showing her what to do as well as telling her why this was necessary. If she complied first time, she was given warm praise. If she did not, then the instruction was repeated calmly followed by a slow count of 'one – two – three', allowing her a second chance to comply. If there was still no response, the staff member gently led her through the required action.

Why it worked

It worked because staff had again thought wider than the simple behaviour – they had considered *why* Molly might be behaving in this way. They planned an approach that allowed Molly to feel more in control of what was going to happen next. They also used methods to teach her to focus her attention and listen, checking for her understanding. All staff members used the '1 – 2 – 3' method consistently so that Molly came to learn that when asked nicely, it is safe to comply – it can even bring a lot of positive attention and praise. When they saw that the methods were beginning to work, they shared them with her parents who managed to help Molly to become happier and more compliant at home as well.

Pulling and tugging

Pen picture

Laura is two-and-a-half. She is a busy little girl who loves coming to playgroup and enjoys playing with the other children there. Her language skills appear to be developing normally, but she is not good at using eye contact or holding a conversation, preferring to talk 'at' people. The problem is that she pulls and tugs at adults when she wants something and has recently begun to pull at other children when she wants the toy they are holding.

How staff worked out what to do

As usual, staff members began with an observation. This gave them all 'thinking time' and helped them hatch a hypothesis as to why Laura was behaving in the way she was. They felt that there were three areas of weakness that they needed to work on. The first was that Laura did not look at another adult or child when communicating with them and so her interactions were very 'one-way'. She also tended to use gestures (pulls and tugs) rather than words. Finally, she was not sure how to negotiate, share and take turns within the group.

What they did

First of all, all staff members consistently used this approach whenever they communicated with Laura. They would use her name, bend down to establish eye contact, and then say what it was they had to say. When Laura spoke to them, they would also establish eye contact, guiding her chin gently to look at them if necessary and praising her for looking at them.

Opportunities were found to share little conversations throughout the session, perhaps in the book corner or with the puppets, in which Laura was helped to see that talking involved 'my turn – your turn'. Staff members looked for play activities that also involved reciprocal interaction – rolling a ball with another child, blowing bubbles for another child to burst, rolling trains to each other, etc. One game was played every single session – a tea party game in which the adult helped Laura to ask each of her friends if they wanted tea and to serve them in turn with plenty of pleases and thank-yous.

Staff members also taught Laura to say 'excuse me' if she needed them and they would hold her hand reassuringly whilst she waited more patiently for them to finish speaking with someone else. After these interventions, staff knew that Laura had become more skilful at social interaction and they were able to show her and then praise other ways of asking for attention or a toy without pulling and tugging.

Why it worked

This worked because staff members did not proceed as if Laura was being 'naughty', but worked out why she might be behaving in this way and taught her the skills she would need to behave otherwise.

Establishing eye contact is a vital skill to learn when communicating – the briefest of eye contacts is always used to signal when it is your turn to speak and when you have finished. This keeps a conversation flowing and allows each of you to pick up all kinds of non-verbal information as well. Gradually Laura was able to behave as if other people were social beings and not simply tools to give her what she needed. Teaching social skills is an important part of the Early Years Foundation Stage framework and should always accompany your behaviour management strategies.

Running off

Pen picture

Carly is three and loves to run about at great speed. Her mother finds it hard bringing her to nursery in the morning as she refuses to hold hands and runs off ahead. Mum is very worried about her safety. Carly seems to have no awareness of danger or boundaries. At nursery, she will make a beeline for any open door and will try to run off if staff members are not vigilant. Mum has asked the nursery staff to help her overcome this problem and is keen to work with them. However, she doesn't know where to start.

How staff worked out what to do

Carly's key person walked home with them one day just to see how bad the problem was. It was clear that Carly did not listen to her mother and that the worry about running off was just part of the problem – Carly's behaviour was disorganised and she had not learned to link cause with effect.

They felt that they should do some work on helping Carly to listen to and follow through instructions first. The manager was concerned about safety aspects and carried out a risk assessment of the security system in the building.

What they did

The manager made sure that security locks and procedures were all in place and that, at all times, there were at least two sets of closed doors between Carly and her 'freedom'. Notes were put up for parents and carers to make sure that doors were always closed on arrival and departure. A key person than began to play alongside Carly, extending her play and concentration, and helping her to play more constructively and imaginatively. Carly loved these sessions and began to watch out for her key person and become more fully involved in their play together.

The key person began to focus her listening skills, using her name and eye contact to 'tune her in' and making sure she had understood what was being said.

After a week or two, the key person had another walk home with Carly and her mother. This time, the key person explained the rules to Carly: 'If you do as you're told, you can walk without holding hands. If you do not, you will have to hold hands. When we are near the main road, you must always hold hands'. She showed Carly which parts of the walk home needed hands and which did not. Where it was safe, she set Carly little challenges to see if she could listen: 'Run to that tree, then wait . . . *good girl!*' This kept Carly focused and occupied for much of the journey. One more walk was shared – this time with Mum setting the rules and challenges and the key person praising Carly. The occasional 'top up' of help from this staff member was offered if needed.

Why it worked

Carly turned out to be a real 'doer' (rather than a 'looker' or a 'listener') and clearly needed much support and encouragement to develop her attention skills first of all. Once she had begun to anticipate and to imagine in her play, it became a lot easier to focus her. At that point, the work on her running away had a chance of being more effective. Working in partnership with Mum and sharing progress in front of Carly gave added 'weight' to the approach and allowed Carly to see that they were all working together. Mum felt better supported and more confident because of this. The staff members offered 'top up' if needed – this meant that they were determined to see the approach through to its successful conclusion.

Scratching and gouging

Pen picture

Josie is nearly two. She enjoys the company of the other children around her but does not yet have any idea about how to interact or to share. While this is not unusual for her age and stage, the problem is that she scratches and gouges at the faces of children who come near her. Staff members have noticed that she does not look cross when she does this – she studies the other child's reactions intensely, almost with an 'academic interest' as if curious about what is happening. She has no concept that she is causing pain and has even been known to laugh after a particularly painful incident.

How staff worked out what to do

Staff members realised that Josie was still very young and that it would not be appropriate to think of her as being 'naughty'. At the same time, it was essential that they planned an intervention since other children were at risk. The problem had been going on for over a month despite their usual approaches (clear rules and praise for gentleness) and so they knew it was more than a passing phase. They asked the manager to arrange extra cover for an hour, so that one of them could play beside Josie to make sure she did not hurt anyone and to introduce a range of situations, such as trying to share toys, sharing lively play, close proximity with other children, coping with not getting her own way, etc. The other staff member carried out a S.T.A.R. analysis (see page 9).

The focus of the observations was on Josie's attempts to scratch and gouge. Staff worked out that the triggers were (a) when Josie was excited (during rough-and-tumble play) and (b) when she felt that her space was being invaded by another child and felt threatened by this at a time when she was enjoying the undivided attention of an interested adult.

What they did

For a short while, a key person was assigned to play alongside Josie and opportunities were created to teach the words 'gentle', demonstrating the action with dolls and each other. Josie loved these sessions and became more interactive with her key person. The staff member then began to introduce play that was more fun with another child and it was suggested that Josie should show or pass toys to the other child, with support and encouragement to keep it successful. The staff member used simple words to show that she was making other children 'happy'. Natural opportunities were also found to introduce the word 'sad' with simple explanations.

Gradually other children were introduced to the play with Josie being given clear rules and shown how to pass and accept toys. If she made an attempt to hurt, there was a clear 'no scratching' and she was immediately removed from the group for a short while, losing the attention of the adult who gave comfort to the other child. Josie was then led back as the helper explained that Josie was sorry and Josie was redirected onto another activity.

Why it worked

Children at this age and stage have little idea about the effect their behaviour has on others and can react to protect themselves in primitive ways, sometimes being fascinated by the response (and therefore continuing to try the behaviour another time simply because it kept life interesting and 'worked' for them).

Through her key person, Josie came to learn that social play could be just as interesting. If she made an attempt to scratch or gouge, this immediately caused the end of the interaction rather than the start of all the interesting play. This method probably worked because staff combined a behavioural approach with a developmental one.

Soiling

Pen picture

Jake is four. He is dry by day, but often has slightly soiled pants which staff members and other children can smell. He never empties his bowels at school and Jake's parents told the teacher that he likes to have a nappy on each evening and hide behind the sofa to do his business. Thus he has never had the experience of emptying his bowel into the lavatory. His mum says that, whenever she tries to make him, he screams and looks frightened. He can 'hold on' for days and not empty his bowels at all if she insists on using the lavatory or a potty. Jake's parents have asked the staff to help them and have promised to take him to their GP if there is no progress in the following month.

How staff worked out what to do

Staff worked with the school nurse who was able to help them work out that Jake had 'overflow soiling'. He was, in fact, very constipated and the slight soiling was seepage from an otherwise blocked gut. She explained to staff and parents that, whilst he was so blocked up, it would be quite painful for him to empty his bowel and he clearly felt less frightened in the privacy of his hiding place. It was clear that Jake did not feel comfortable with the idea of dropping a bowel motion, preferring to pass it into a nappy.

Staff also wondered if there had been a great deal of anxiety surrounding his difficulty and whether this anxiety had, in fact, made the problem worse. So they decided that a light-hearted and positive approach was needed. They knew Jake to be a sensitive, imaginative little boy and decided to use this strength to engage his interest in toileting success.

What they did

The school nurse met with parents and provided a diet sheet for Jake, making the most of those healthy foods that he already enjoyed – fruit, breakfast cereals, fruit juice and brown bread. Staff met with parents to agree this approach and proceeded with their permission and full knowledge of the method used.

Jake sat with his key person and his mother in a quiet area with a supply of paper, coloured felt-tip pens and collage material. The staff member told the story of 'Mr Pongo Poo' and invited Jake to draw him, drawing many chuckles as he did so. As he drew, he was told the story of Mr Pongo Poo who lived in Pooland and had to get home each night to the rest of his family (which Jake duly drew). This progressed over several short sessions, with Jake taking home his artwork to share with the family. After a couple of sessions, Jake was invited to send Mr Poo home to Pooland and actually agreed to 'have a go'. By this time, his diet was having some effect and the motion was easy to pass. His father had arranged an extra surprise – as Jake pulled the chain, the effect was almost like Disneyland – Dad had put glitter, food colouring and soap solution into the cistern!

Why it worked

This kind of therapy is based on the principle of helping children to externalise problems and therefore deal with them better. The story of Mr Pongo Poo gave Jake a context in which to see what was going on and allowed him to move on from his entrenched situation. The approach could not have worked had not the school worked closely with his parents – neither would it have been appropriate to deal with a sensitive matter such as this without their full involvement. Medical advice was needed at some level, and you should always ask parents to arrange a visit to the GP first to check for constipation, diet and any other medical condition. The final surprise reward from Dad was 'the icing on the cake'!

Spitting

Pen picture

Liam is a lively three year-old. He attends a nursery class for the mornings and is collected by his childminder at lunchtime where he is cared for during the afternoon along with another little boy. Liam has recently taken to spitting and this is especially bad when he is at the childminder's. Apparently this is not a problem at nursery though his mother has found that he spits at home as well – especially when he is being cheeky to his mum. He has also made a game of spitting down staircases, encouraging other children to join in and laughing hilariously. Whilst everyone recognises that this is a passing phase, it is an unsociable habit that the childminder wants to break quickly.

How the childminder worked out what to do

With Mum's permission, the childminder contacted the nursery teacher to ask about his behaviour there. Apparently, Liam did spit for a few days, but this was dealt with assertively ('we don't spit at children here') and he quickly stopped. His teacher does find that he needs a lot of directing and that she needs to 'stay one step ahead of him' lest he become mischievous or starts to play wildly.

Mum says that when he first spat at his cousins, they all laughed at him and it became a game. She is cross with him when he spits at her though she has also tried an ignoring approach to see if that helped too. The childminder came to the conclusion that (a) Liam needed to be distracted and kept stimulated, (b) he needed to be given clear rules, (c) she should make sure that he did not gain too much attention from spitting and (d) whatever she decided to do, she should do it consistently and link in with home.

What they did

The childminder decided to plan the afternoons with a little more structure so that Liam had plenty to do without resorting to antisocial behaviour. With Mum's agreement, they both decided to use 'time out' for managing the spitting behaviour. Whenever Liam spat, he would be told calmly and clearly 'No spitting' and removed from the activities for three minutes. He would then be helped to return to the play, say 'sorry', and distracted onto a new activity. At first, Liam was invited to choose a large sticker at the end of his childminding session and asked why he had won it: 'Because I didn't spit'.

Why it worked

Younger children (two and under) will spit because of the reaction they get from it. If there is a lot of disgust or laughter, they are likely to repeat the behaviour just for attention. They simply need clear information as to how to behave. However, some older children (three and above) persist and the behaviour cannot be ignored. This particular approach combined four strategies often used in behaviour management. It involved avoiding the situation (keeping him busy), clear rules ('no spitting'), a sanction (brief time out) and a reward (a sticker). The childminder also made sure that he understood what he had done to earn time out and helped him to say 'sorry'.

Swearing

Pen picture

Lol comes into the group happily and likes to play in a boisterous manner. He finds it hard to control his voice and is often shouting loudly at the other children. Unfortunately, much of this shouting also contains swear words. He seems to have no awareness that these are offensive to others, but does seem to enjoy the attention that his swearing brings him, grinning mischievously and repeating the words if challenged.

How staff worked out what to do

Staff members were rather daunted about tackling this problem since they were anxious about talking to Dad about it. Dad himself appeared to have a similar temperament to Lol and staff members were not sure how aware he was that his language could be rather 'rough'. At the same time, they knew that something had to be done because others were complaining and Lol needed to know how to make and keep friends.

They started by establishing a positive relationship with Dad, sharing all the things that Lol was learning to do in the group. They then explained that they would like to work on developing Lol's spoken language 'ready for school' and to help him find appropriate ways of expressing himself when he felt angry or excited. One of their goals was to stop him saying words like . . . (these were stated). Dad, of course, had to agree. Staff members then made the usual observations – when was Lol most likely to swear? (when playing boisterously and when he did not get his own way); what did he actually say?; and what did it achieve for him? (a release of excitement and emotion, also a great deal of attention which put him in a powerful position within the group).

What they did

One staff member spent some time with Lol on a one-to-one basis, working out which words were good words to use in the group and which were not allowed. She approached this in different ways on three different occasions – first 'thought storming' good words and bad words, then helping him to post good words (read by the helper) into the smiley-faced post box and bad words into the sad post box, and then using puppets with Lol as the teacher.

The same staff member modeled to him how to ask properly for toys, how to take turns and how to share over the rest of the session, helping him develop the right words. A 'rules – praise – ignore' approach was then used. Lol was reminded to use good words and praised strongly for doing so. Swear words were ignored as far as it was safe to do so, encouraging other children to take no notice either. A huge sticker at the end of each session celebrated the fact that he had managed to use good words.

Why it worked

Dad might have felt annoyed and defensive if staff had asked straight away: 'Where do you think he learned how to swear?' They made sure that Lol actually knew what words he should be using and what words he should not.

Although adults often feel that children know this only too well, children are only reacting to the responses they get from others and may need much clearer information about how to talk. Once they knew that he understood, staff members were clear to use an ignoring approach (which appears to be the most effective way of dealing with swearing). However, they combined this with a positive teaching approach, making it more fun and attention-getting to speak properly than to swear. They shared their work with Dad who was pleased with progress and became a little more self-aware of how he was speaking at home as well.

Temper tantrums

Pen picture

Marissa is two and has, on average, seven major temper tantrums per session. She presents as an angry little girl who finds it hard to wait for attention, share adult attention with other children and to comply with requests. Staff members are worried that 'she is her own worst enemy' – as soon as there is an interesting activity to do, Marissa appears to spoil it with her temper. They are concerned that she is not getting as much out of her nursery sessions as she could and they are also concerned because of the effect her tantrums have on other children.

How staff worked out what to do

Members of staff used one of their regular staff meetings to discuss Marissa's behaviour. They realised that this was far more than a passing phase and that they needed to plan approaches that were different to usual. They also realised the effect that the tantrums were having on their own emotions – with behaviour like this, the temptation is to feel angry in response and to see the child as being 'naughty'.

Talking to each other helped them to feel less angry and powerless themselves and see Marissa's behaviour more objectively. They agreed that Marissa needed to learn that temper tantrums did not lead to the desired result (more adult attention/getting her own way), but that she also needed to learn that playing socially could be fun and to learn the social skills that went with this. They suspected that Marissa was also an emotionally needy child who genuinely needed a lot of support and attention. Talking together enabled staff to agree in precise words what constituted a temper tantrum for Marissa (screaming, falling down and kicking) and what observations they would gather (using S.T.A.R. observation both for temper tantrums and also for gathering information about activities that went really positively). They also talked with her foster parents.

What they did

The period of observation turned out to be really important as the observer began to 'tune in' to Marissa, her strong emotions and her frustrations. It seemed that she had genuine difficulties in accepting rules and guidelines. It was as if Marissa did not trust the adults around her to be consistent and that she needed to take control herself instead. This was scary for her. From what little the staff knew of her home background (she had recently been taken into foster care), this could well be the case.

The staff chose one of them to be a 'secure base' for Marissa, greeting her each morning and spending individual time with her before joining the group and supporting her. Outbursts were treated consistently with calm containment – removing her calmly and firmly from the group whilst her key person sat silently with her until the outburst had subsided. She was then helped to rejoin the group and supported in a new activity.

Why it worked

The new, more sympathetic way of regarding Marissa's outbursts helped staff members deal with them in a much calmer and more consistent way. There are some children who develop unusual or disordered ways of forming emotional attachments and they tend to move rapidly from calm to extreme outburst with no 'shades of grey' in between, as if they have learned that only severe outburst of emotions is going to secure for them what they need. With the presence in her life of calm, consistent adults who could cope with and contain her outbursts, Marissa began to settle in the group and with her foster family, though it took some time.

Useful books

Mortimer, H. (2001) *Personal, Social and Emotional Development in the Early Years*. Stafford: QEd Publications.

Mortimer, H. (2001) *The Observation and Assessment of Children in the Early Years*. Stafford: QEd Publications.

Mortimer, H. (2002) *Supporting Children with AD/HD and Attention Difficulties in the Early Years*. Stafford: QEd Publications.

Mortimer, H. (2003) *Emotional Literacy and Mental Health in the Early Years*. Stafford: QEd Publications.

Mortimer, H. (2003) *Trackers 0–3*. Stafford: QEd Publications.

Mortimer, H. (2004) *Trackers 3–5*. Stafford: QEd Publications.

Mortimer, H. (2006) *Behaviour Management in the Early Years*. Stafford: QEd Publications.

Mortimer, H. (2006) *Music Makers: Music circle times to include everyone*. Stafford: QEd Publications.

Mortimer, H. (2006) *Controlling your Fireworks: Managing anger in young children*. Stafford: QEd Publications.

Mortimer, H. (2006) *Worry Box: Managing anxiety in young children*. Stafford: QEd Publications.

Mrazek, M. & Garrison, W. (1993) *A-Z Guide to Your Child's Behaviour*. London: Piccadilly Press.

Sutton, C. (1999) *Helping Families with Troubled Children: A Preventative Approach*. Chichester: John Wiley & Sons.

Woolfson, R. (2004) *Why do kids do that?* London: Hamlyn.